MW00484473

Leadership In Everyday Life
IT REALLY IS ALL ABOUT YOU

Mary Raymer
LMSW, ACSW, DPNAP

and

Gary Gardia
MEd, LCSW, CT

Strategic Book Group

Copyright © 2011
All rights reserved – Mary Raymer, LMSW, ACSW, DPNAP
and Gary Gardia, MEd, LCSW, CT

No part of this book may be reproduced or transmitted in any form
or by any means, graphic, electronic, or mechanical, including
photocopying, recording, taping, or by any information storage retrieval
system, without the permission, in writing, from the publisher.

Strategic Book Group
P.O. Box 333
Durham CT 06422
www.StrategicBookClub.com

ISBN: 978-1-60976-550-7

Printed in the United States of America

Book Design: Rolando F. Santos

To Natalie Raymer,
for providing the kind of leadership that inspired me
to be a better human. Her life was the epitome of resilience,
good humor and the challenges and rewards
of looking within.

— Mary —

To my lifetime role models,
my father and mother, Ed and Irene Gardia.
What amazing examples they are of leading the way
through life's challenges.

— Gary —

Acknowledgements

We want to thank the every day leaders who find their courage within like Susan, Bob, Carol, Kay, Laura and Diane in this book. They move and inspire us.

Thank you also to Dennis McClure, Darlene Cross, RuthAnn LaMott, John Schneider and Martha Huffman for their guidance and support.

Much gratitude goes to Kathy Brandt for encouraging us and making us better.

And finally a very special thanks to Kim Schropp for her support and her tireless work in the preparation of this book.

Introduction

The Wonderful/Awful Truth

Contrary to the opinion of many people, leaders are not born. Leaders are made and they are made by effort and hard work.

— Vince Lombardi —

Legendary Head Football Coach of the Green Bay Packers

Do you sometimes feel like you are all alone in the world? Do you question the purpose and meaning of your life? Perhaps you wonder what happened to your optimism and energy. Maybe you feel that people around you are taking advantage of you or not thinking about your needs. If you feel any of these things you are certainly not alone. Many people feel out of control in their everyday lives and in society at large. People report feeling more stressed, less certain of their future stability and like they are struggling as opposed to thriving.

There is a thirst for effective leadership. People spend literally millions on self-help books every year looking for a pathway to happiness. Too often pop psychology dwells on the external forces that purportedly define and wound us as opposed to examining and enhancing the internal forces that we actually command. Frequently, the message given is that we are victims and our behaviors are not our fault. We are told to stop beating ourselves up and then provided with a certain number of steps to take in order to attain personal success and happiness. These books often sell well for awhile and peddle wonderful promises of transformation. Like eating junk food, they provide temporary fulfillment but soon we are back to our own devices and on to yet another self-help book. The bottom line is that it is far too easy to blame others for our internal misery. Certainly, we have all had hurt in our lives. Of course there are many external forces that we do not control, but victimhood is a chosen and debilitating state. Whatever traumas, losses or difficulties we face, we can choose how we respond. Is it easy? Sometimes it is and often it isn't, but the point is, remaining a victim often produces disastrous results.

All too often we find excuses for our poor behavior. The more we rationalize, blame and judge, the worse we feel. Imagine what might happen if we were to stop that pattern.

Naturally, when we are hurting we grieve our losses and disappointments. It is understandable that we feel out of control and question our beliefs. We may even wish that someone could magically fix our life for us and lead us out of our distress. Well, we have some good news for you. That someone is you.

Right this minute you have the power to learn from your experiences and move forward. While victims stay trapped by their pain, leaders have the courage to look deep within, face the truth and move ahead. When you are a leader in your own life you have the courage to continually question and challenge yourself. You have the courage to be wrong and change course. Leaders are open to learning about themselves and others while continually striving to do their best even, and especially, in the face of adversity. Leadership is a choice, not a job title. When you are a leader in your own life and act out of your best self you live a life guided by values and ethics. Your behaviors are consistent with the character traits that are important to you. When you slip up, as everyone will, you promptly take responsibility and rectify your mistakes. Becoming a leader in your own life is crucial to building resilience and self-esteem.

No matter where you are in life, you can be effective as a leader. You can take yourself and others to destructive places or healthy places. You can take the strengths you already have and build on them. You can acknowledge your vulnerabilities with compassion and reduce your judgment and criticism of yourself and others. The first step is to accept the fact that choosing to remain a victim cripples you. We all have pain and loss in our lives. We all have experienced hurt and disappointment at the hands of others. Whether you experience terrible damage or great growth remains within your control. How will you choose to address it, as victim or leader?

What does it mean to be a leader in your own life? That is what this book is about. To be a leader in your own life means not waiting for others to change or admit their mistakes. It certainly doesn't mean waiting for someone to finally give you the key to reaching nirvana. It means managing the aspects of your life that you control and letting go of the need to control everything else. Being honest with yourself and others and taking responsibility for your life can lead you to where you really want to be. When you give attention to growing healthy behaviors and thought patterns, the way you experience life changes for the better. This change creates an environment that encourages those around you to grow in meaningful ways also. It means challenging yourself to engage in problem-solving rather than feeling defeated by problems. Good critical thinking as opposed to negative thinking helps you identify the real problem, brainstorm potential solutions, develop a plan and then take action. It also means if that plan doesn't work you choose another course of action and try again.

Leadership in your own life will be illustrated in this book by identifying six key concepts for healthy living. The key concepts include: leading with our values; finding the courage to act; using personal insight to identify our strengths and challenges; building flexibility; managing our minds; and using mortality as a motivator. Each story highlights one particular concept. This is not a quick fix book but a starting point in a lifelong process. There are no magical answers, but there are realistic and effective ones. That is the wonderful/awful truth. Work lies ahead and great rewards are possible. This book is about self-examination, character building and becoming the kind of person you want to be. It is about challenging yourself not to coast through your life.

As therapists who work with people at the end of their lives, we see too many people who have regrets because they feel they have wasted so much of their potential. They often say they wish they could relive even some of their worst days prior to their terminal illness. They say they would have risked more, felt more and had the courage to fail more. Unfortunately, too many people also see that they didn't lead themselves to the places they really wanted to be. There is an incredible opportunity here; wake up before you hear you are dying. We hope you can challenge yourself to move your life forward to the places you really want to be by being your best self. To this end, the authors have created a companion workbook that will guide you through 12 monthly lessons that include key concepts from this book as well as problem solving, personality conflicts, critical thinking, planning for change and staying on course.

For information about this companion workbook visit www.leadershipineverydaylife.com.

In the following chapters, you will be reading the stories of six ordinary people and how at critical points in their lives, they chose the path of personal leadership. They took control of their lives and didn't wait for someone else to lead the way. They show us what we are all fully capable of achieving – becoming leaders in our own lives.

This is the true joy of life, the being used up for a purpose
recognized by yourself as a mighty one; being a force of nature
instead of a feverish, selfish little clod of ailments and grievances,
complaining that the world will not devote itself
to making you happy.
— George Bernard Shaw —
Irish Playwright

Chapter 1

Values: A Map To Alaska
Won't Get You To Nebraska

Personal leadership is the process
of keeping your vision and values before you
and aligning your life to be congruent with them.
— **Stephen Covey** —
American Author and International Speaker on Leadership

The very act of striving to live our values is a powerful force in our lives. Our personal code of ethics, or lack of one, is the key to shaping our decisions, behaviors and, ultimately, our character. If we can articulate our values and then, more importantly, define what it would look like if we were basing our actions on them, we would have a road map for life and enhanced self-esteem. Living our values requires the ability to resist some of our questionable, albeit human, impulses and choose healthier, more responsible actions. Espousing values but not living them drains our self-esteem, energy and negatively impacts our relationships. If we say we value honesty but we lie about our actions, we feel the weight of our own hypocrisy. When our actions are more in line with our values we feel better about ourselves and find more joy and reward in everyday life. We also learn that we can trust ourselves to do the right thing even when we fall into unhealthy patterns or behaviors. Working on living our values helps us make corrections more quickly. Every time we choose to do the right thing, we enhance our confidence in our ability to take care of ourselves no matter what comes our way. This provides a healthy and realistic sense of power and control in our everyday lives. We do not control all that occurs in our lives, but we do get to choose what we do next.

Susan was a divorced 45 year-old woman who woke up one morning and knew she had to change her life. Petite with intense brown eyes and dark black hair, she observed the extra forty pounds on her body with disdain. She was tired of waking up every morning with a headache and feeling lonely and agitated. Susan's husband left her two years ago for his 25 year-old administrative assistant. Susan, who had been a non-drinker until then, started drinking shortly after her husband left the house. She drank at night and on weekends to the point of passing out. At first she told herself that it was temporary and just to help her sleep. She tried to stop several times but returned to drinking. She wanted to knock herself out. She never missed a day of work but increasingly started missing social commitments. She felt abandoned, hurt and angry. She obsessed over every detail of her husband's betrayal. The alcohol was the only thing that eased her pain and loneliness.

No one knew Susan was self-medicating. Her friends and coworkers thought she was stressed out and tired because of the divorce and needed her space. None of them had ever seen Susan drink too much because she always drank at home alone. Susan knew she was rationalizing and justifying her behavior because of what her husband had done. The more she drank the more she felt everybody had abandoned her; she kept spiraling down into bitterness. Previously, she was upbeat and positive. She loved nurturing her family and friends. In fact, that was a driving force in her life…to bring comfort and joy to others. Now, she felt disappointed in everyone, but especially herself. She missed social occasions and personal milestones like birthdays of people she cared about. She was either too hung-over to attend or started drinking before the event and didn't want people to see her under the influence. When people were sick she used to be first on the scene with soup or bread but now she couldn't muster the energy to get involved. Guilt was her constant companion. She had always valued a healthy lifestyle. She had watched her nutrition and exercised religiously. Over the last two years she had let it all go. She knew she was not the woman she wanted to be. She despised the self-pity she dragged behind her day in and day out.

When she missed her first day of work because of her drinking, she promised herself she would take her life back. She made a list of what still mattered to her. First she had to address the alcohol which she knew was sucking all the energy out of her life. Her physical and mental health had to come first.

Susan gave a lot of thought to what she had taught her daughter growing up, as well as to what she wanted for her daughter now. She knew her daughter, like everyone else, would face disappointments and losses in life and she certainly wouldn't want her daughter to self-destruct the way she herself was doing now. Susan decided she wanted to be a role model, not a horrible example of how 'not to be'. She started reading up on alcohol and women's health. The link between alcohol and depression was very clear and she knew she had to stop drinking, not just for physical reasons, but for mental clarity as well. First she started exercising again. Slowly but surely she forced herself to walk a little longer every day after work instead of rushing home to drink herself into oblivion.

She made a commitment to treatment for her alcoholism and quit drinking completely. She exercised regularly and

3

took time to make nutritious meals. She reached out to her friends again. She worked hard to stop obsessing over how her husband had hurt her. She knew she had been hurt and changed by his betrayal but she also knew obsessing over it only kept her stuck. She recognized that she could decide how the divorce would change her; either she could stay a victim or move forward into a new and healthy life. As she started taking responsibility for making positive changes, the shame she had previously felt began to ease. She started taking new risks and felt hope again. She was still sad that her marriage had ended but did not obsess over it.

Contributing to the greater good had always been important to Susan. Drinking and isolation had stopped her from participating in these activities. She made a list of causes that really mattered to her and chose to focus on environmental issues. She started to volunteer with a local land conservancy. Her focus and self-esteem continued to grow. She was becoming the person she really wanted to be. At times she was still lonely, but she also felt exhilarated by the opportunity to rebuild a life that was consistent with her values. As she moved on with her life she continued to maintain a healthy lifestyle. Even though she thought she could never trust a man again, she eventually was able to and committed to a healthy, loving relationship. Again, that wonderful/awful truth – ultimately Susan realized that the quality of her life was up to her. She could choose to stay miserable or she could choose to revise her life using her values as a guide.

Lessons Learned:

What have we learned from Susan that we can apply to leadership in our everyday lives?

1. The first step to redesigning the direction of your life is to define your values and prioritize them.

    Too many people allow impulses, urges and feelings to determine the actions they take. This is a scattered and inconsistent approach and rarely gets you to the self you want to be.
    When you define the values you believe are most important, you have a target to shoot for that keeps you moving in a positive direction.
    When you get lost or confused you have touchstones to bring you back into balance. When Susan made a list of what really mattered to her she began the process of finding her way to a better life.
    Prioritizing your values refines the process even more. Feelings are mercurial and based on numerous variables. They often are not fully based in reality. Good critical thinking helps you make choices that are based on your values and not your feelings.
    You no longer give your power away to other people's reactions when you use your values as the landmarks to measure your progress along the way to a better life.

2. Living your values takes persistence and energy.

    It is often much harder to live your values than you think it will be. If it were always easy, you would feel no sense of growth in how you feel about yourself.
    When you make choices that are consistent with your values you do not need to hide from yourself or

others. Your decisions make sense to you. You don't just go along with the crowd if other people disagree. The map of your values guides you through the everyday choices that shape your character and the quality of your life. When Susan took steps to live her list of values, her self-esteem grew.

3.   The ability to articulate your values is the first step to becoming your best self, but translating those values into concrete steps is where the real transformation is achieved. You need a plan of action.

The list of your values is an important starting point for taking charge of your life. It is, however, only a starting point. Like Susan, we all need to define what matters, but then we need to define what we would be doing if we were living accordingly. Making a plan and breaking things down into concrete actions is crucial.

- What are the key values you want to guide your life?
- What is the most important value of all?
- What would it look like if you were to live that highest value in a consistent manner?
- How would you treat yourself and/or others differently?
- How are you already living this value in your life?

Leaders strive to live their values to the best of their ability. This is the key to enhancing the quality of your life. When life throws you disappointments you have more resilience because, rather than obsessing, you devise coping strategies and action plans based on what matters most to you. You have a road map to guide you. When you don't live your values, you feel discomfort, guilt and shame. Values coupled with courage are essential to being a leader in your own life. In the next chapter we will look at how courage helps us move forward with the inevitable ups and downs that we all encounter.

We do not act rightly because we have virtue or excellence, but rather, we have those because we have acted rightly.

— Aristotle —

Greek Philosopher

Chapter 2

Courage: Running Into The Mouth Of The Lion

It takes a lot of courage to release the familiar and seemingly secure, to embrace the new. But there is no real security in what is no longer meaningful.

— **Alan Cohen** —

Author, *Chicken Soup for the Soul*

How would your life look if you always had courage when you need it? The inability to overcome our fears prevents our lives from being the best that they can be. Fear keeps us stuck in places we believe to be safe even when we know this safety is a barrier to true happiness. Yet it is a mistake to think that courage is the absence of fear. Courage means taking the high road, and taking risks even in the presence of fear. What would your life look like if you were not blocked by fear?

Bob was a balding and overweight 53 year-old man who had been married to his wife Carol for 35 years. They began their lives together as childhood sweethearts and married when they were both 19. They raised two children who were now 20 and 18 years-old and away at college. At this point in their lives both Bob and Carol would describe themselves as best friends, yet Bob started to feel unsettled. While being married to his best friend felt nice, he found himself wondering what happened to the romance. He also began feeling that his job was not rewarding and noticed he had an overall sense of boredom in his life.

Bob started inviting friends to meet up at a neighborhood sports bar a few days a week after work. They would watch whatever game was playing on the big screen, share some laughs and drink. During these times Bob felt better because, as he said, "I was finally having some fun again."

As Bob started coming home later and later, Carol decided to work on a college degree. While she was not pleased that Bob was staying out late these evenings, she trusted in his faithfulness to her and was actually grateful for some time to pursue her longtime interests. Carol became very excited about all the things she was learning and buried herself in her studies.

As a result, Bob began feeling abandoned and angry. In response, he spent even more time away from home with friends and at his favorite hang-out. He started criticizing Carol to his friends. It was easy to convince others that she had lost interest in him and abandoned their marriage for college. Bob referred to it as her attempt to regain her youth. His friends began encouraging him to consider a divorce and offered to set him up with someone who would appreciate such a good guy. Bob thought if Carol really loved him, she should make the first move to repair their relationship. She never did.

Up to this point, Bob was a person who typically blamed other people for the difficulties he experienced. He was in good company. On many occasions he spoke with friends about his problems. The stories he relayed always supported the fact that he was the victim. His friends did the same with their life stories, so they felt a sense of camaraderie.

Then one day Bob worked up the courage to ask the tough question, "What has been my role in this?" While Bob really wanted to see Carol as the cause of all the problems, he realized several areas of his life were in trouble, and he needed to look at himself as the source. He found that to be excruciatingly painful. He went back and forth between thinking, "It is not me, it is her," followed by, "But I love her, I know who she really is and I want *that* person back in my life." This final thought always meant he had to ask himself the essential question, "Could the problem be me?" Clearly, this option would lead to pain for Bob, and the easy way out would be to avoid this line of thinking at all costs.

Bob decided it was time to have a serious conversation with Carol. He did not want to take full responsibility for all that had happened and he knew something had to be done. He asked Carol out to dinner and began talking about his regrets. While there were some rough moments and several difficult weeks to follow, things started to get better.

Bob committed to coming straight home after work. The problem was that Carol had developed a life away from Bob that she was not ready to give up. At first Bob felt resentment, "I went through all of this torment, confessed my sins and now you are not giving up everything and running back to me? I knew this would happen and I am out of here." But then Bob would regain focus on his highest priority, a healthy and loving relationship with Carol. He realized he had spent much time looking at this situation before they spoke and that Carol was essentially hearing about it for the first time. He decided he was responsible for the shift in how they defined their relationship. It would be up to him to become the person he wanted to be with Carol, without attachment to how she had to be in return. He knew he had to lead by example and was ready to do just that. While the solution was clear to Bob, the work continued to be a struggle for months to come. Eventually Bob and Carol were able to discover a new and positive way to be with one another. Leading with courage and insight, their relationship and marriage evolved over time as did their happiness together.

11

Lessons Learned:

What have we learned from Bob that we can apply to leadership in our everyday lives?

1. Many times in life we are blocked by the challenges we face. When obstacles present themselves we always have a choice. We can do what seems safe and easy or find the courage to face obstacles head on. In some situations it seems so much easier to avoid the truth rather than take responsibility for our actions.

    For Bob, it was much easier, at first, to hang out with his buddies and then blame his wife for the distance they both felt. Bob's lie was mostly to himself; he wanted to believe Carol had abandoned their marriage for college when, in fact, it was Bob who initiated the distance first.

2. We have learned that courage is acting with integrity even in the presence of fear. Leaders are often faced with having to make tough decisions such as:

    *   Speaking up or remaining silent.
    *   Taking responsibility for their actions or blaming someone else.
    *   Finding a way to remain true to their values or ignoring what is happening because it is easier to do nothing at all.

    Bob showed he was finally able to muster the courage to look inward and then speak up in order to mend the damage he had caused. He was able to take a leadership role in turning the marriage around and getting it back on track.

3. The way your life looks is the result of the choices you have made up to this point.

- We all know someone who has stayed in an unhealthy relationship too long because they were afraid to speak up or take action.
- Sometimes we stay in jobs that are demeaning or compromise our integrity because we are afraid to make a change.
- There are times when we waiver on our personal values out of fear that doing the right thing will have painful consequences.
- We put off making positive changes in our lives such as changing careers in order to earn more money, addressing behaviors such as addictions, or even confronting friends who have a negative impact on our lives.

The critical question to ask ourselves is, "How might my life look if I was not blocked by fear?" If you examine the list above you might be able to say, "It is not fear that blocks me. I just don't want to feel uncomfortable." Fear in this context can range from mild discomfort to outright terror. It is important not to deceive ourselves here. Even overcoming our discomforts takes courage.

At the beginning, Bob was afraid of being wrong. He did not want to admit he was responsible initially for the distance created in the marriage. Later on, Bob was afraid of speaking up because he did not want to face Carol's response. Marriages end every day because someone does not want to speak up and tell the truth… and then it becomes too late, the damage is done.

4.   Blame does feel good, at least in the moment. We often deceive ourselves by saying the words, "It is not my fault," feeling as if we have been absolved of all responsibility, and thinking along these lines:
- First: "It is not my fault."
- Second: "Then it must be out of my control."
- Third: "If it is not in my control then there is nothing I can do about it."

We have taught ourselves that by being helpless and not in control we are, at least theoretically, off the hook for the way our lives evolve. The more we engage in this type of thinking, the more difficult it becomes to turn our lives around. Once we figure out this pattern, we have the option to change course. We do that by finding the courage to take responsibility for our lives and tackling life's challenges head on. Here are some thoughts to help you get back on track:

- If you lack the skills you need, find a way to get those skills. We live in an age where information abounds in places such as public libraries, community education programs and the internet.
- Conduct an assessment of where you are in your life. Create a plus/minus list of the things you like and the things you do not like. Take a look at the role you have played in both areas.
- Make a plan to address the important items on that list and see where you need to take responsibility for negative outcomes.

In addition, while we have acknowledged that leadership is not always easy, there is one thought that has helped many folks when faced with tough choices:

take progressive steps. If you cannot tackle a problem or a challenge in one fell swoop, don't give up. In many cases, some movement forward is a great place to start. For example, it would be wonderful if alcoholics would just stop drinking. For many struggling with addiction, this thought is not only paralyzing, it often leads to an escalation of their addiction. Seeking assistance, telling the truth about their behavior, or even telling a friend can be the first step towards positive change.

Here are some thoughts about taking progressive steps:

- See if you can remove blame from the equation and look at the simple truth about what is occurring.
- Develop a plan and begin in a place that feels safe to you.
- Take some forward action.
- Evaluate your progress and take the next step.

This book is about leadership. Leadership, by definition, is about our relationships with others. Finding a way to become a role model for others is an important goal for leaders. Setting a positive example for the people in our lives is not always an easy thing to do and often takes great courage. It also takes an understanding that leadership really is all about you.

In the next chapter we will look at how the way we perceive ourselves can help or interfere with being a leader. Do we see ourselves as superior and everyone else as inferior? Do we see ourselves as victims of the world around us? In either case, it would be difficult to be effective as a leader.

The greatest barrier to success is the fear of failure.
— Sven Goran Eriksson —
Swedish Football Manager

Chapter 3

Personal Insight: So Back To...
It Really Is All About You

I shut my eyes in order to see.

— Paul Gauguin —

Leading Post-Impressionist Painter

It is difficult to become effective as a leader in any area of life without engaging in objective self-assessment. How can we lead others if we cannot lead ourselves? There are many examples of people in important leadership positions whose personal lives have been in shambles. In most of these cases, it all seems to implode at some point. Today, when you turn on the news you will see example after example of people who preach one thing yet live another and eventually lose it all. Is that because they feel they are exempt from the rules they believe others should live by? Or maybe they hold the belief, "I am a good person no matter how I behave," without engaging in some form of regular self-assessment.

It is easy to justify our own behaviors by ignoring them or by claiming temporary insanity. Without personal insight we will continue to believe our thoughts, actions and behaviors are somehow disconnected from their outcomes. Let's see how the concept of personal insight played out in Kay's life.

Who would have ever guessed that Kay, a tall and elegant looking woman, 32 years old with blonde hair and green eyes, was uncomfortable around other people or that she was unhappy? By all indications she was content with her life. Working as a nurse at the local hospital, coworkers were frequently heard saying, "Kay is the best nurse we have." She was committed to advocating for patients and their loved ones and she had excellent nursing skills. She also appeared to have great courage when fellow staff members needed someone to speak up against management, particularly in meetings. When in the company of others, Kay did that very well. Following meetings, she often received kudos from her previously silent coworkers. They would say things like, "Boy, you really told them off!" and, "You aren't even worried about losing your job! I really admire you for that." This type of praise felt good to her.

Even though she received all this praise, there were problems. Kay had times when she was angry and became impatient with coworkers and even, worse, with patients. People seemed to disregard her outbursts. They believed this exceptional person must have good reasons to get upset so they gave her the freedom to continue her behavior. Her supervisors were aware, based on experience, that reprimanding Kay meant not only facing her wrath, but also the anger of her fellow employees. "How could you treat Kay like that? You know she is the only person who will stay late and no one works as well with difficult patients," they would say. It was becoming obvious that Kay was able to influence the dynamics of the entire unit. If she was in a good mood, so was everyone else. If Kay was in a bad mood, things were not good for anyone.

Finally, Jane, one of Kay's coworkers, decided it was time to come clean. She asked Kay to lunch and shared her thoughts and feelings about the negative effects of Kay's behavior. Jane highlighted several key points:

- Kay had to be right all the time and that made her very difficult to work with.
- Kay assumed she was speaking for all her coworkers in meetings when, in fact, she was not.
- Kay was not receptive to feedback of any kind.

Kay was devastated. Now feeling that people were ganging up on her, the worst of her behaviors began to escalate. Eventually, after several complaints from patients, Kay was fired from her job.

During the next couple of weeks, Kay came crashing down to the very foundation of her self-identity. She realized that maybe, just maybe, she was at least part of the problem. She asked herself, "Who am I and what have I become? Could I be so wrong about how I thought my life was going?" She began to realize her lack of personal insight was the obstacle to her happiness. Her all-consuming need to be right led to losing good friends and the job she loved.

"How could this have happened to me?" Kay found herself saying out loud. As soon as she spoke those words she instantly felt as if someone had thrown scalding water on her. "Happen *to* me? As if I was just standing around minding my own business and I accidently tripped on myself! This wasn't something that just happened to me," Kay thought to herself, "I created it! I started by believing my own press. People put me in the position of being 'the best nurse we have' because I would not allow them to say anything different. Look at how I behaved. I was not the best nurse. There were others who went about their work quietly and professionally and who were highly skilled and effective. They were better than I was in many ways." Kay began to realize her unwillingness to look at herself honestly had become a destructive force in her life.

Kay moved on with her life and quickly found another

job. She continued to struggle with her need to be right. At times, feedback of any kind felt threatening but she was able to change her reactions and behaviors. By engaging in some very difficult self-assessment she reached a place of honest personal insight. She could now focus on developing an improved sense of self and live her life with more integrity.

Lessons Learned:

What have we learned from Kay that we can apply to leadership in our everyday lives?

1.   Kay would not allow herself to be wrong in any way and deep inside she had decided she would rather be right than happy. That is exactly what happened. While her professional life fell apart she was able to continue to tell herself that she was right and everyone else was wrong. For a short period of time, those thoughts brought Kay some degree of comfort, but she quickly realized she was not happy at all.

     Effective leaders are able to:

     - Give and receive personal feedback. When we are committed to higher values (in this case, quality patient care in Kay's workplace) it is important to speak openly with one another about what we are doing well and where we can use improvement.
     - Look honestly at their strengths and vulnerabilities and develop strategies to become their best selves.
     - Lead others to do the same through personal example.

2.   Kay was off-base about who she believed she was. She was also off-base about what others thought of her. Sometimes our sense of who we are is on target and sometimes we miss by a mile. Being wrong about who we believe we are can have disastrous results.

3.   Kay finally figured out her role in creating the problems she experienced and she took action to change. Developing a realistic sense of self requires us to pay attention to who we are, how we think and how we affect others. From this perspective it really is, once again, all about you.

4.   Kay continued to struggle. Lifelong patterns can be difficult to break. How we see ourselves and, in turn, how we behave can be deeply rooted in patterns that have developed over many years.

Personal insight is a process that requires constant attention and the ability to see objectively who we are, how we think and how we act.

- Take a moment to think about a couple of people you know who do not like you. If you could get an honest answer about why they do not like you, what would they say? Would there be any truth in their responses?
- Now think about people you know who like you very much. What would they say about you? Would their responses be 100% factual?
- Keep in mind that other people don't know everything about you; how would you describe yourself?
- Where do you exaggerate or stretch the truth about who you are?

- Based on your responses to these questions, what do you see as your leadership strengths and where could you use improvement?

In the next chapter we will look at the importance of flexibility in our lives. The more flexible we can be, the easier it is to remain objective about any situation. Then we can lead based on facts and not in response to the drama around us.

A moment's insight is sometimes worth a life's experience.
— Oliver Wendell Holmes —
American physician, poet, writer, and professor at Harvard

Chapter 4

Flexibility: Gumby Had It Right

Blessed are the flexible, for they shall not get bent out of shape.
— Chuck Gallozzi —
Canadian author, speaker, seminar leader, and coach

Mental health might very well be summed up with one word: flexibility. The more flexible we are, the more likely it is that we will bend instead of break. Flexibility is not about becoming passive nor is it about compromising our values.

"It is what it is," Jeff was fond of saying. "We spend so much time complaining about things that cannot be changed, we lose sight of what is important." Jeff was a 28 year-old accountant who worked at a large financial institution. About 5'6" tall, he was shorter than many of the other men he worked with, but because of his self-confidence, people said he appeared taller. Growing up as the middle child in a very large family, Jeff had learned the fine art of keeping the peace. He also had a sense of calmness about him and an uncanny ability to defuse tense situations. One of ten members of an accounting team, Jeff was not the manager of his department nor did he want to be. He was happy with his job and enjoyed his work.

Signing an initial contract and accepting a paycheck meant to Jeff that he had a responsibility to do the best job he could for his employer. Yet staying true to this value was difficult where he worked. Many of his coworkers focused more on their personal desires and what was wrong with the company than with the health and well-being of the organization. At first this was just a bit of an annoyance for Jeff but then things got worse.

One Friday afternoon the manager called everyone together and announced there would be significant changes ahead. Four members of their team would be laid off and their work redistributed among the remaining six employees. Jeff was not among those to be released from their duties. The manager also informed the group that those who remained would have to figure out among themselves how to get the work load completed. She expected the team to be back on schedule by the end of the following week. While several members of the team took the opportunity to voice their concerns, the manager let them know the decision was not negotiable.

If employee morale was low prior to the layoffs, it had now reached toxic levels. Instead of working toward a solution to the challenges they faced, the employees now focused on demonizing management. Monday and Tuesday of the following week came and went with no progress toward redistributing the workload. People were angry and took every free moment to express their resentment. While tempted to join in with this negativity, Jeff knew that would not be productive. He still believed his job was to do whatever he could to make the company successful whether or not he agreed with its decisions.

He knew it was time to step up and see what he could do to turn things around. Wednesday morning Jeff got everyone together to share his thoughts about the situation.

He began the meeting by acknowledging the anger and frustration the group was feeling as well as their fear of losing their jobs.

There was agreement from everyone in the room. "So let's talk about our options at this point," Jeff said. "I have given this a lot of thought; let me see if I have it right." He proceeded to make the following points:

"We can do nothing at all and go back to our jobs feeling victimized and resentful. I don't know about you, but not doing anything does not work for me. I do not like feeling powerless and I would rather not continue on the path we have been on for the past few days. We have been getting nowhere and making ourselves miserable. Agreed?"

"We can tap into our anger, put together a petition and let management know we will not tolerate this kind of treatment. I know this was what most of us were thinking when we came to work this morning. We can let management know we are angry but that is not likely to be effective."

"We can take the challenge we have been presented and put together the most productive and effective department this organization has ever seen. Yet why in the world would we want to do that?" Jeff asked the group hypothetically. "While it might temporarily feel good to find a way to sabotage the department, is that really who we want to be? We are friends here and we know each other well. I know that deep down inside each of us have values that would not allow us to do that."

For several minutes the teammates talked about their options and agreed they would feel some regret if they disregarded their values. "So that leaves us with one option," Jeff said. "Let's show management we can get the job done. Whatever happens next, we can always say we maintained personal and professional integrity through some very difficult times."

Lessons Learned:

What have we learned from Jeff that we can apply to leadership in our everyday lives?

1.   It is easier to remain flexible if your values are clear.

Doesn't it feel good at times to get even (or even plan to get even) when we feel we have been wronged? Yet when we stop and examine our values, getting even drops off the list of options. In this case, Jeff quickly realized the organization did not belong to him or to the members of his team. They were all hired to do the work that was assigned to them. While they had the option to leave if they felt their integrity was being compromised, they did not have the right to undermine the department. Jeff helped his team find more flexibility by making it clear they all had a shared higher value and that was integrity.

Values and flexibility go hand in hand. If our values are clear and strong but we are not flexible, then we develop a rigidity that can prevent us from seeing all possible options. If we are flexible but we lose sight of our values, then the options we explore will likely be misguided.

2.   The sign of a true leader is remaining flexible in the face of change.

In the end, Jeff and his team chose to take positive action rather than react negatively. Certainly, they had made an effort to speak up but when they were told the decision was final they decided to make the best of the situation. Leadership and flexibility go hand in hand in the following ways:

- There is power in being flexible. Flexibility allows us the opportunity to maintain a clear focus on what is most important in order to make the best possible decisions.
- When we are flexible we are constantly looking for new skills and new ways to approach problem-solving.
- Flexibility allows us to look at change as a challenge instead of an obstacle or a personal attack.

3.   We do not have control over most events that occur in our lives but we do control how we react to them.

When a spouse unexpectedly tells us they want a divorce, when we are faced with layoffs in the workplace, or when we discover we have a serious illness, we first feel out of control. That is normal and expected. Feeling angry, resentful and even numb would also be typical, but just because feelings are normal does not mean they should determine what we do next. A flexible and resilient response would be to feel whatever we are feeling without judgment but then find ways to move forward with life the best we can, bringing our feelings along with us. That is not as easy as it sounds, yet choosing a self-destructive path only makes things worse.

So how flexible are you? How well do you cope with change?

- Do you feel you are able to see most changes as challenges instead of obstacles?
- Are you able to find humor even in tough times in order to remain positive?
- Are you able to stand back and look at challenges objectively in order to figure out the best option?

- Are you usually able to make the best of difficult situations?

The good news is that flexibility and resilience can be practiced and improved. One way to remain focused on maneuvering positively through tough times is to stick close to your values.

In the next chapter we will explore how the way we think can influence the way we feel and behave. Looking at how to recognize and redirect faulty thinking is an essential skill for leaders in all areas of life.

The boldness of asking deep questions
may require unforeseen flexibility
if we are to accept the answers.

— Brian Greene —

American theoretical physicist

Chapter 5

The Importance Of Managing The Mind:
I Think...Therefore It Is

How much easier it is to be critical than to be correct.

Benjamin Disraeli

Former British Prime Minister and Author

The lens through which we view our world has a profound impact on our ability to function effectively. We all have random and reactive thoughts and feelings. We also have the ability to determine if they are based in reality or in some way distorted. We can ask ourselves if the content of our thinking is helpful or harmful. When we balance our thoughts we have the power to change how we feel about ourselves, others and situations in our lives. Many people have learned negative thought processes which magnify difficult feelings and block creative problem-solving. When we magnify the negatives in our lives, jump to conclusions, personalize life events that are not personal or see things in black and white categories, we trap ourselves mentally. Our feelings respond accordingly. It is like the difference between throwing gasoline on a fire instead of water. We may indulge in the type of thinking that views negative events as persistent bad luck or wonder, "Why me?" These thoughts pull us down and make us feel like victims. Our other choice is to talk back to these negative thoughts and say, "Why not me?" The sooner we address 'what is' and challenge ourselves to make healthier choices to deal with situations head on, the sooner we will feel energized and more hopeful.

Laura was a 31 year-old mother of 2 year-old twin boys and a 7 year-old daughter. She worked part-time as a receptionist at a law firm and was well respected by her peers. She was married to her high school sweetheart who had a business as a handyman.

Externally Laura seemed to have a wonderful life but internally Laura was anxious and frequently felt inadequate. Even with her many accomplishments she always felt like she wasn't good enough. She minimized the positives and magnified the perceived negatives in herself, others and her life in general. Her husband often expressed frustration that she couldn't relax and enjoy all the good things about their life together. One day he broke down and told her he didn't know how much longer he could handle her criticism. He did not want to leave her but he said her negativity was exhausting. He felt he could no longer fix enough things about himself to make her happy. He said no matter what he did, he didn't feel like it was acceptable to her. He also worried about the effect her attitude was having on their children. Last but not least, he said that she was becoming her mother even though she had said she never wanted to be like her.

Laura was shocked by this revelation. The message that haunted her the most was that she was becoming like her mother. Laura was an only child whose mother was a rigid and critical perfectionist. Laura would frequently hear that she would never amount to anything if she didn't lose weight, work harder, be nicer, etc. Her mother was short-tempered, driven, and full of dire predictions. As a result,

Laura thought there was nothing she could do to be good enough.

Laura was stunned by the parallel between her husband's words and her childhood thoughts. She remembered well the black and white thinking that caused her suffering; either she was perfect in her mother's eyes or she was a total failure.

Years before, during a particularly nasty bout of feeling worthless, she had purchased a book by David Burns, M.D., that talked about faulty thinking and the relationship between thoughts and feelings. She pulled it out and this time, really concentrated on the content. The more she read the more she recognized how her thinking patterns were magnifying her negative feelings. Her whole perception of reality was distorted. There were many good things in her life, yet she focused on the negative and deprived herself of any possible enjoyment. She began to identify the ways her thoughts could create anger, anxiety, depression and strained relationships in her life.

Laura was amazed by how many of her faulty thinking patterns were similar to her mother's. Frequently jumping to conclusions, over-generalizing, minimizing the positives and maximizing the negatives...these and more became clear. Laura took the advice of a friend who was a social worker and started writing out her thoughts, especially when she felt particularly anxious, angry or depressed. When something disappointing occurred she saw that, instead of saying to herself that the situation was disappointing, she turned it into the worst possible thing that could have occurred. On top of that, she blamed herself or someone she was in a relationship with for this failure. She began to see how, even when good things happened, her thoughts would badger her by saying, "It should have been better." Over time Laura learned to test reality and balance the messages she gave herself. Her relationship with her family improved and she began to enjoy life more.

31

Lessons Learned:

What have we learned from Laura that we can apply to leadership in our everyday lives?

1. Listening to your thoughts and balancing the messages in your mind helps you make better choices.

    Balancing the messages in your mind is very different from the simplistic concept of positive thinking. Unrealistic positive thinking or Pollyanna thinking does not work; you are not naive. Obviously, everything in life is not positive nor will it work out according to your plans. Balanced thinking helps you acknowledge that, while events in your life may not be ideal, perhaps they are not as awful as you think. Even if events are pretty bad, you still have a choice as to how you view them – as challenges or defeats. When you view a situation as a challenge you rally your internal energy and are able to start problem-solving. You look for what is possible and take steps to get there. If you are defeated in your own mind before you get out of the gate, you don't even try and then fall into the victim trap.
    - Self-respect grows when you weigh the pros and cons, choose a plan of action, implement that plan and see how it works.
    - The more you trust yourself to do the best you can, the more confident you feel in your ability to handle whatever comes your way.
    - If your plan didn't work you can try a new strategy; if it did work you can have an internal celebration.
    - Either way you are an active participant in your own life and not at the mercy of events and faulty thinking.

2.   Your thoughts can either help you or hurt you.

Faulty thinking that is not corrected can doom you to repeat patterns that are self-destructive and unproductive.

- Faulty thinking hurts you and can also hurt the people you care about. Faulty thinking can have disastrous results in your life and in the lives of people who are important to you.
- Unrelenting negativity stops you from finding viable and creative solutions to life's challenges.
- You begin to feel like you think and your negativity becomes a self-fulfilling prophecy.

3.   How you think is a learned pattern, not an inevitable personality trait that cannot be changed.

Thought patterns are learned behaviors, therefore you can unlearn the faulty thinking that paralyzes you or drives you in unhealthy ways. Culture at large and your family of origin often teach you ways of thinking, usually unintentionally and by example. The negative thoughts feel like the truth, so you may not recognize them at first. The good news is, once you catch them you are able to correct them. For example, rather than saying, "I am a failure," you can say, "Well, I am certainly not perfect but I do many things well. As for things that I don't do well, I will learn from them and keep working on them."

- Look at your patterns of thinking.
- Are they based in reality?
- Would you say such things to a loved one?

Once Laura started listening to what she was really saying to herself, she was able to take charge of her life again. While everything and everyone stayed the same, changing the vantage point positively affected all areas of her life.

If you are going to be an effective and positive leader in your own life you need to ensure that you are not reacting to negative or faulty patterns of thinking. Leaders are able to step back, identify and acknowledge their feelings and test the reality of their thoughts so they can make better and more rational choices.

We do not have forever to get to where we want to be. The role of mortality as a motivator will be explained in the next chapter.

Negative thinking is always expensive – dragging us down mentally, emotionally and physically.

— Peter McWilliams —

Best Selling American Author

Chapter 6

Mortality As A Motivator:
Is Death Really The Enemy?

Death is not the greatest loss in life.
The greatest loss is what dies inside us when we live.

— **Norman Cousins** —

American Political Journalist and Author

Many people don't make out wills, appoint a durable power of attorney or make their wishes known regarding end-of-life medical care until the very last minute, if at all. The notion that avoidance is a talisman against death is quite common. What do you think our lives would look like if we could live each day fully aware of our limited time on the earth? Would we live differently? Would we savor things more and have more gratitude for what we have? Would we be more effective at achieving the goals that really matter to us? The experience of healthcare practitioners suggests that it would indeed make a difference. It is not uncommon for people with a serious illness to express a strange gratitude for their terminal prognosis. The nearness of death has the potential to create sadness and wisdom simultaneously. It can motivate people to make changes in

35

their lives before it is too late.

Diane was a 45 year-old dentist. She was a stunning woman with beautiful red hair and blue eyes. At almost six feet she had a regal bearing and cool composure. She had a few friends but they rarely found time to spend together. Diane's only living family was her husband who was an emotionally abusive alcoholic. He refused to seek counseling of any sort. Diane was resigned to the fact that she would be unhappy in love. She had taken her wedding vows very seriously and did not see divorce as an option.

One beautiful sunny day Diane went for her annual mammogram. The next day she received a message from the health center calling her back for another mammogram and possible ultrasound. Her mind raced. She could visualize herself in a turban and sitting in a chemotherapy room all alone. She kept reminding herself that getting called back for a second mammogram is common and usually nothing to worry about. Unfortunately, this time it was something to worry about. Diane had advanced breast cancer with lymph node involvement that had metastasized to the bone.

Diane felt terribly alone and frightened. She was seeing her life crystallize in front of her eyes and there was clearly a choice to be made. She could succumb to depression or she could fight to have a better life regardless of how long she had to live.

Diane found her courage. She felt a strong urge to do something different with her life. She always wanted to volunteer for a hospice in her community but had kept putting it off. She knew physically and emotionally it would be too difficult to work directly with others who were seriously ill, so she worked in the office at the outpatient unit as a receptionist. The courage didn't stop there. She knew she was enabling her husband to self-destruct by staying in the marriage. As terrifying as it was to her to be alone and living with breast cancer, she set an ultimatum. Either he got help for his alcoholism and they initiated marriage counseling or she would divorce him. He chose alcohol over the marriage and she followed through with the divorce. While this was a difficult and painful decision she also began to feel a new respect for herself.

Diane found volunteering at the hospice program both incredibly gratifying and frightening. Seeing her future in the faces of the patients there motivated her to keep moving toward her best self and a better life. She reached out to old friends and began developing new friendships with fellow volunteers.

Eventually she became a patient of the hospice she served and her old and new friends created a circle of care. The volunteers she had worked with loved her dearly and she felt like she had a real family for the first time in a long time. By setting herself free from an abusive relationship, she was able to engage in genuine and loving relationships. Diane chose to live as fully as possible for as long as possible and her choice inspired everyone who came in contact with her.

Lessons Learned:

What have we learned from Diane that we can apply to leadership in our everyday lives?

1. Not addressing your mortality can keep you in a constant state of procrastination. Awareness of mortality can paralyze you or motivate you. Ultimately, that is your choice.

    *   How often do you say, "One day I will fix my life or beat that addiction or be more gentle with my mother?" Why not today?
    *   You can move forward with positive behaviors more consistently when you acknowledge that you don't have forever to live.

- Moving forward knowing our time is limited can create a more meaningful life.

2. Confronting death can motivate you to become your best possible self. Awareness of our limited time can push us to act on our priorities, which in turn creates richer lives. Rather than living in denial and wasting precious time moving down ineffective or destructive paths, you can focus your energies on meaningful actions and behaviors.

   - Becoming your best self requires proactive behavior.
   - Denial of mortality gives the illusion there is always plenty of time. We don't have forever to change our ways. Now is the time to fix our lives and live our values.

3. Confronting mortality helps you live your life more fully. Living your life fully does not mean living your life irresponsibly. It does not mean doing whatever you want whenever you want and doing so without regard for others. Quite the opposite, it means taking full responsibility for your life.

   - Look realistically at what currently works in your life and what doesn't.
   - Identify some concrete goals based on changing what doesn't work.
   - Identify how making better choices enhances your integrity and your character.

Diane became a leader in her own life. By changing how she lived she inspired those around her who witnessed her quiet courage. Many friends and volunteers who were privileged to watch Diane's transformation reevaluated how they were living their own lives. They looked at where they were stuck and where they were not in synch with their own best selves. Diane was a leader by example. While she never set out to be a leader, what a powerful one she was.

I am convinced that it is not the fear of death, of our lives ending, that haunts our sleep so much as the fear…that as far as the world is concerned, we might as well have never lived.

— Harold Kushner —

Rabbi and Best Selling Author

Summary

The Leader You Need Is You

You can and should shape your own future;
because if you don't someone else surely will.

— **Joel Barker** —

Author and Originator of the Concept of Paradigm Shifts

We have created a culture that is so narcissistic that the phrase "It is all about me!" has caught on like wildfire. As human beings we have a natural tendency to focus on survival by putting our own needs first. There are times when this is appropriate. But when we shove others out of the way in order to be first in line or disregard the feelings of others, we are tapping into the ugly side of our survival instinct.

In this book we have learned what leadership is and is not. Leadership is not:

- Bullying or 'guilting' others into living the way you think they should.
- Taking the easy path in order to appear successful or avoid conflict.
- Lying so that others will not think less of you.

- Putting up a false front in order to gain the respect of others.
- Staying in unfulfilling situations in order to avoid the pain of change.
- Seeking power for the sake of bolstering ego.

Leadership is:
- Being clear about your values and vision and making choices accordingly.
- Influencing others positively by how you live your life.
- Developing healthy relationships.
- Engaging continually in self-assessment in order to avoid becoming either over or under confident.
- Living with courage.

As we have read through these chapters, we have learned some valuable lessons from people who have demonstrated effective leadership. Granted they are not in situations that would make front page news, but they are in situations we all might face in our everyday lives.

Susan was the divorced 45 year-old woman struggling with alcoholism. She taught us the importance of seeking help, telling the truth, setting goals and staying on track, but most of all, she taught us the importance of leading with our values. Ayn Rand said, "Happiness is that state of consciousness which proceeds from the achievement of one's values." Susan began her journey by examining her values and prioritizing them. She then realized that success included the failures along the way and did not let those failures take her off course. True leaders are clear that they could end up in the wrong place if they are not using their values as a guide. Planning with constant attention to what is most important ensures that our 'map to Alaska gets us to Alaska'.

From Bob, the 53 year-old husband of Carol, we learned the importance of courage. Bob demonstrated courage by telling the truth about who he was and mistakes he made. We have probably all been in situations where it seemed easier to just let things go, not fully realizing that as each day passes, more and more damage is created. It takes courage to speak up and ask, "Can we stop and talk about what is going on here?" True leaders understand that in many situations fear is the barrier to achieving positive results and courage is the way past fear.

Kay was the 32 year-old nurse who taught us the importance of self-assessment and the role of insight into how we think and act. How easy it is to go through life thinking that all our problems exist because of someone else. We think, "If the world would just cooperate with me and my plans, my life would be incredible." An easy way to see if your thinking is in any way similar to this is to look at how you think and act while driving a car. Are you a person who thinks the 'waters should part' when you enter the highway? True leaders understand how easy it is to deceive themselves into believing they are something they are not, either over qualified or under appreciated. They are clear about the importance of engaging in objective self-assessment.

From Jeff, the 28 year-old accountant, we learned the importance of moving through life with flexibility and resilience. Jeff could have easily joined in with his coworkers, feeling victimized by management. Instead he chose to stay focused on leading with integrity. True leaders are able to remain flexible in the face of life's most difficult challenges.

Laura was the 31 year-old mother of three children who taught us how the way we think can interfere with our happiness. Many of us engage in faulty thinking. It is sad to think that we could spend years of our lives in undue distress when, by changing the way we think, things could have been better. True leaders are aware of faulty thinking and how they can use it to convince themselves they are right.

True leaders are able to detect these patterns in themselves and redirect their thoughts so they make better decisions and choices.

From Diane, the 45 year-old dentist, we learned the value of treasuring every moment of life. When Diane was diagnosed with a serious illness, addressing the fact that her time was limited became difficult to avoid. In essence we all share Diane's struggle; our time is limited, too. We don't know exactly how much time we have left. Elizabeth Kübler-Ross said, "Live each day as if it were your last and one day you will be right." How would you live your life if you knew you only had a few months left to live? Why do we wait to live fully and with passion? True leaders understand that time is limited and precious and not to be wasted.

Take a moment now to consider the following:

- Do you acknowledge that your time is limited? Do you use that thought to motivate yourself and others to live life fully and with passion and excitement?
- Do you allow fear to block you from going after your dreams?
- Are you able to stand back and take an objective look at your strengths and weaknesses and put together a plan for self-improvement?
- How flexible and resilient are you with the challenges that arise in your life?
- Are you aware when you engage in faulty thinking?
- What is your plan for your future?

Thomas J. Watson said, "Would you like me to give you a formula for success? It's quite simple, really. Double your rate of failure. You are thinking of failure as the enemy of success. But it isn't at all. You can be discouraged by failure or you can learn from it, so go ahead and make mistakes. Make all you can. Because remember that's where you will find success."

Leadership in everyday life is not a goal to achieve but a way to live. Some days we will do a better job of it than others. That doesn't matter. What does matter is that we remain clear about our values and stay focused on leading ourselves and others to a place of better living.

Leaders establish the vision for the future and set the strategy for getting there; they cause change. They motivate and inspire others to go in the right direction.

— John Kotter —

Harvard Business School professor

For information about Leadership in Everyday Life two day intensive workshops, workbooks and ongoing educational opportunities visit www.leadershipineverydaylife.com.

LaVergne, TN USA
07 March 2011
219196LV00001B/37/P

9 781609 765507